CLONE WARS

ADVENTURES

VOLUME 7

designers
Darin Fabrick and Josh Elliott

assistant editor
Dave Marshall

editor
Jeremy Barlow

publisher
Mike Richardson

special thanks to Sue Rostoni, Leland Chee,
and Amy Gary at Lucas Licensing

The events in these stories take place sometime
during the Clone Wars.

www.titanbooks.com

www.starwars.com

STAR WARS: CLONE WARS ADVENTURES Volume 7, March 2007. Published
by Titan Books, a division of Titan Publishing Group Ltd., 144 Southwark Street,
London SE1 0UP. Star Wars ©2007 Lucasfilm Ltd. & ™. All rights reserved. Used
under authorization. Text and illustrations for Star Wars are © 2007 Lucasfilm Ltd.
No portion of this publication may be reproduced or transmitted, in any form or by
any means, without the express written permission of the copyright holder. Names,
characters, places, and incidents featured in this publication either are the product of
the author's imagination or are used fictitiously. Any resemblance to actual persons
(living or dead), events, institutions, or locales, without satiric intent, is coincidental.
Printed in China

4 6 8 10 9 7 5

STAR WARS®

CLONE WARS
ADVENTURES
VOLUME 7

"CREATURE COMFORTS"
script and art **The Fillbach Brothers**
colors **Ronda Pattison**

"SPY GIRLS"
script **Ryan Kaufman**
art **Stewart McKenny**
colors **Dan Jackson**

"IMPREGNABLE"
script **Chris Avellone**
art **Ethen Beavers**
colors **Dan Jackson**

"THIS PRECIOUS SHINING"
script **Jeremy Barlow**
art **The Fillbach Brothers**
colors **Ronda Pattison**

lettering
Michael Heisler

cover
The Fillbach Brothers and Dan Jackson

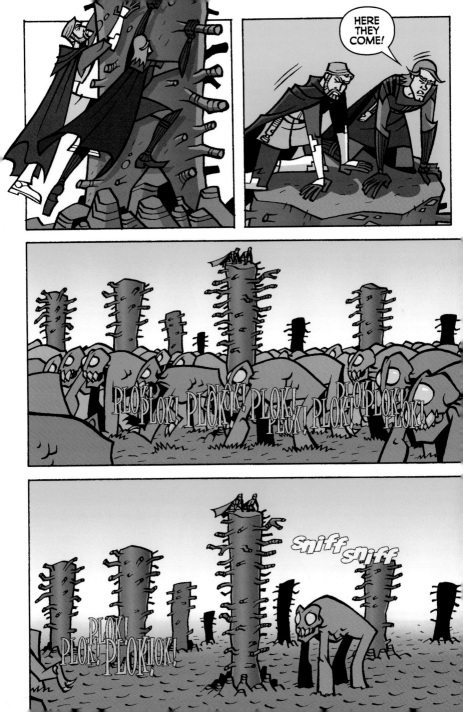

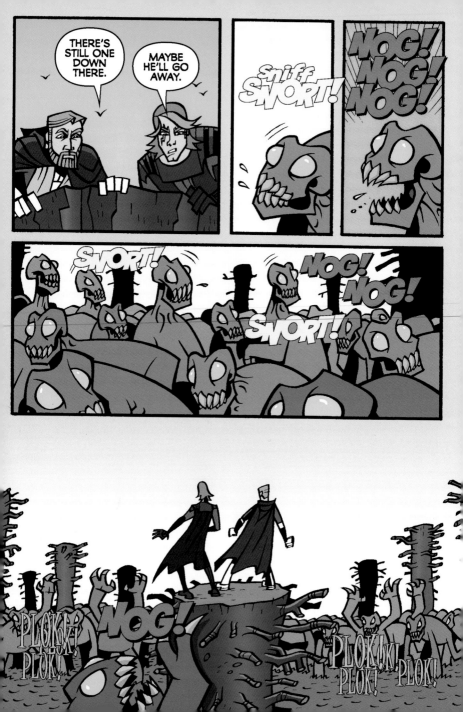

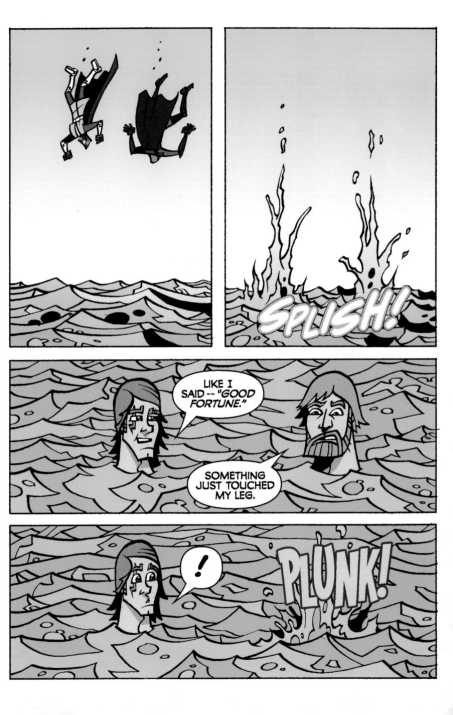

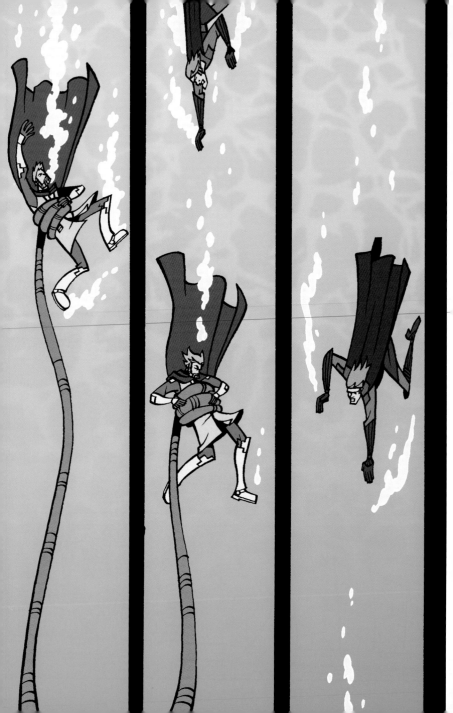

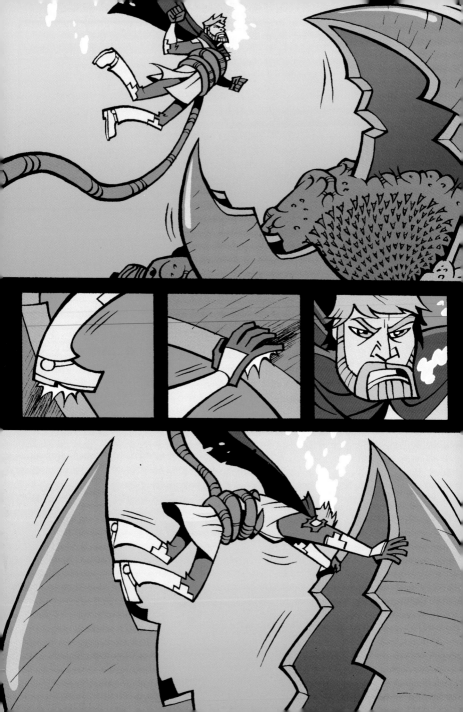

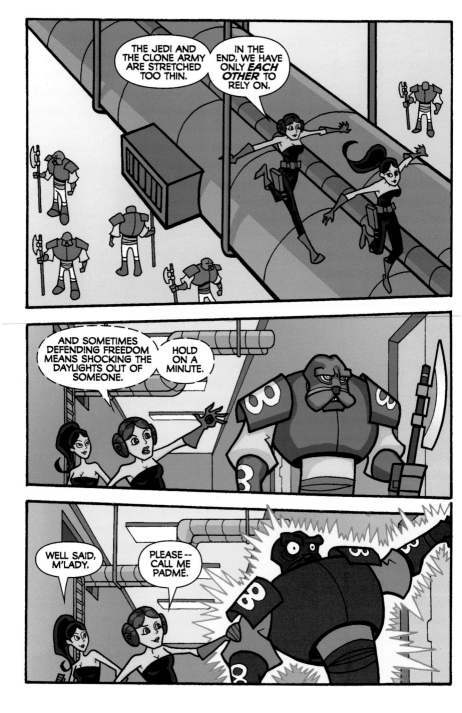

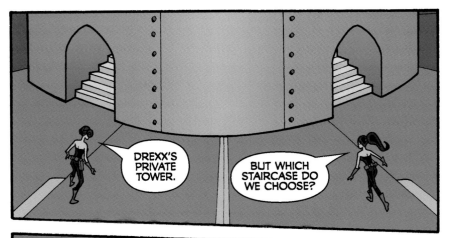

GAAAAHHH!

THEN AGAIN, WHY SHOULD THE BIG BOYS HAVE ALL THE FUN?

GRRRR! GET BACK HERE!

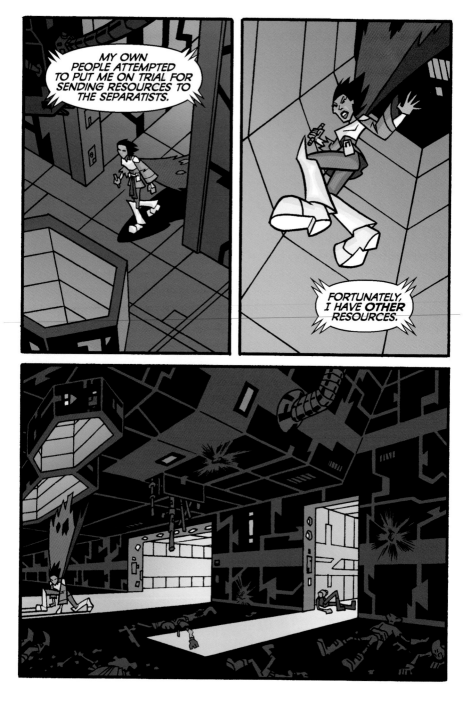

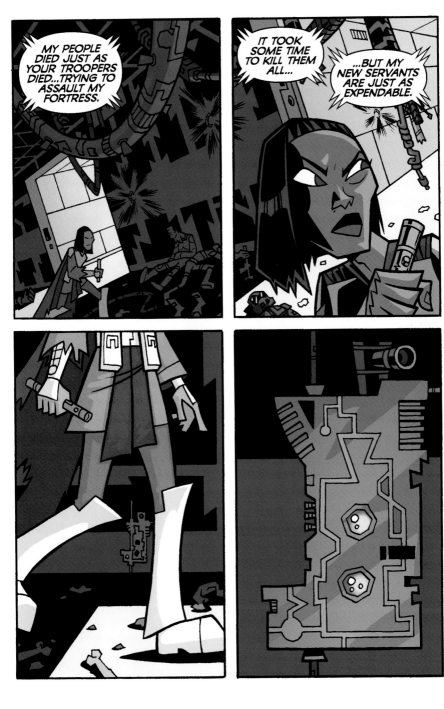

AND HERE YOU ARE. YOU CAN'T GET IN, YOU KNOW-- AND *THIS* IS THE ONLY ENTRANCE.

THE DOOR IS TOO THICK FOR YOUR LIGHTSABER TO CUT THROUGH, AND IS MAGNETICALLY LOCKED.

VVMMMMM!!

THE MECHANISM IS TRIPLE-CODED AND...

IT'S *THIS* WAY! YOU COULDN'T FIND YOUR WAY OUT OF AN AIRLOCK!

I'M GONNA THROW *YOU* OUT OF AN AIRLOCK!

THE VAULTS ARE *THIS* WAY.

I SHOULD'VE LEFT YOU TWO IN THAT FIELD...

NO, I SHOULD GET *TWO* OF THOSE CANNONS -- THEN I'LL HAVE SOMETHING TO SHOOT AT!

WAIT... ...I *KNOW* THEM.

TRILLAN KATOS AND HIS FAMILY. HE AND I WORKED AT THE BANK TOGETHER FOR YEARS.

THEY'VE HAD ME OVER FOR DINNER. MORE THAN ONCE.

THOSE VAULTS WON'T WAIT FOR US.

IF WE DON'T KEEP MOVING, THE TREASURE WILL BE GONE...

...AND OUR HOPE FOR ESCAPE ALONG WITH IT.

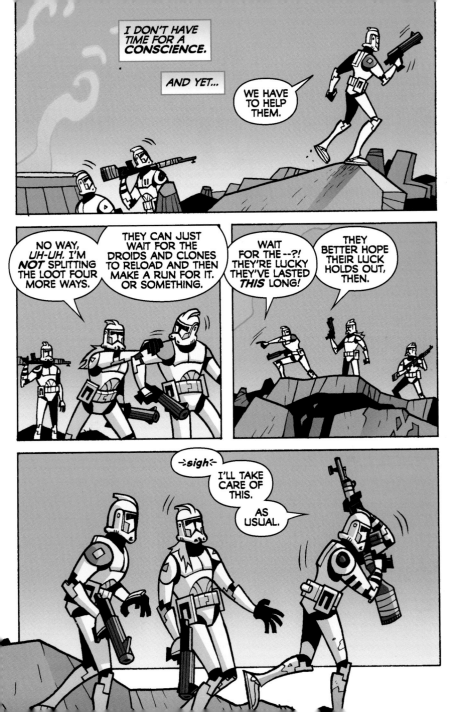

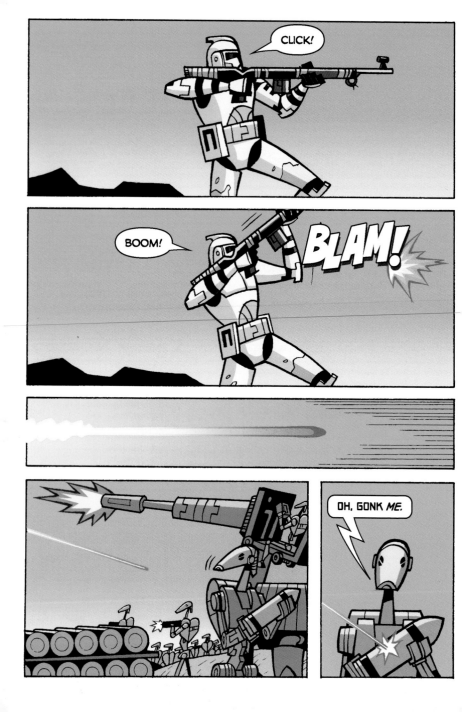

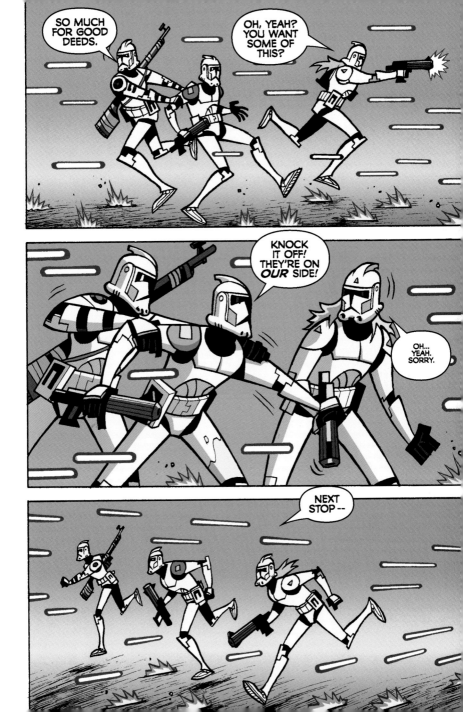

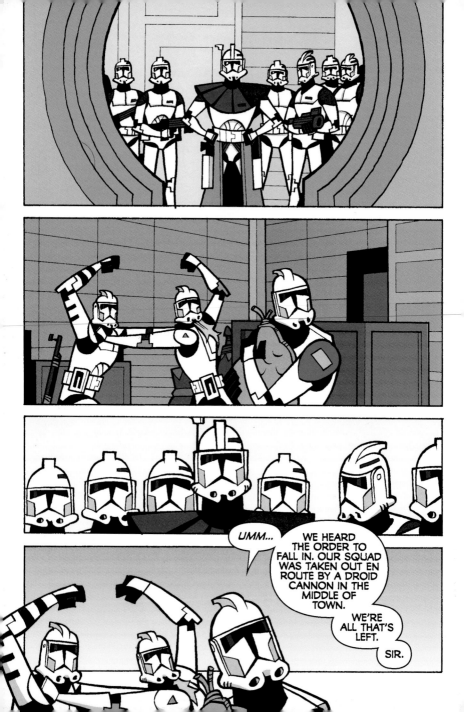

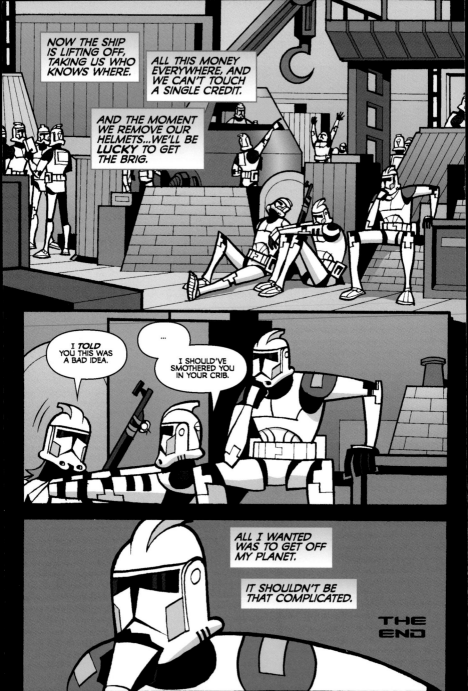

STAR WARS

TOP TRUMPS®

They're out of this world!

and now play Star Wars
Top Trumps on your mobile!

To Shop, Play and Win online visit

TOPTRUMPS.COM